PARAMAHANSA YOGANANDA
(1893–1952)

IN THE SANCTUARY OF THE SOUL

A GUIDE TO EFFECTIVE PRAYER

PARAMAHANSA
YOGANANDA

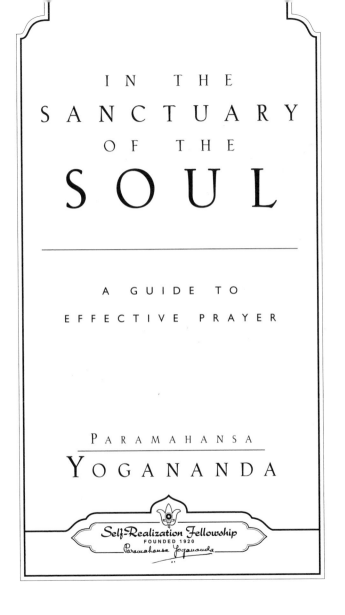

Self-Realization Fellowship
FOUNDED 1920
Paramahansa Yogananda

ABOUT THIS BOOK: *In the Sanctuary of the Soul* is a compilation of extracts from Paramahansa Yogananda's writings, lectures, and informal talks. These selections originally appeared in his books, in articles in *Self-Realization* (the magazine he founded in 1925), in the three anthologies of his collected talks and essays, and in other Self-Realization Fellowship publications.

Authorized by the International Publications Council of
SELF-REALIZATION FELLOWSHIP
3880 San Rafael Avenue
Los Angeles, California 90065-3219

The Self-Realization Fellowship name and emblem (shown above) appear on all SRF books, recordings, and other publications, assuring the reader that a work originates with the society established by Paramahansa Yogananda and faithfully conveys his teachings.

First edition, 1998; This printing, 2013

ISBN-13: 978-0-87612-171-9
ISBN-10: 0-87612-171-7
Library of Congress Catalog Card Number 97-62489
Printed in the United States of America
1620-J2658

CONTENTS

Preface

By Sri Daya Mata (1914–2010), third president
and spiritual leader of Self-Realization Fellowship/
Yogada Satsanga Society of India

I met Paramahansa Yogananda in 1931, when he came to my hometown of Salt Lake City to give a series of lectures and classes. It was a meeting that profoundly transformed my life.

Though still a teenager, I was seeking spiritual answers. I had listened to the sermons of various church ministers; but my heart remained unsatisfied: "Everybody talks about God, but is there no one who actually knows Him?"

When I entered the packed auditorium where Paramahansa Yogananda was speaking, the spiritual upliftment, power, and love radiating from his presence instantly convinced me — to the core of my being — that I was in the presence of one who had found God and could guide me to Him.

One night he spoke on faith and will power. He so inspired me that as I sat and listened to him I felt it was definitely possible to move mountains with faith in God.

When the lecture was over, I waited to greet him. I had been suffering for quite some time from severe blood poisoning throughout my system — the result of an accident in high school — and the doctors could find no cure for it. During our conversation, he suddenly said to me, "Do you believe that God can heal you?" His eyes were alight with divine power.

I replied, "I *know* God can heal me."

He touched me in blessing on the forehead. Then he said, "From this day forward, you are healed. Inside one week your scars will be gone." And that is exactly what happened. Within one week the condition had cleared, and has never returned.

For Paramahansa Yogananda, faith and prayer to God were not a matter of wishful thinking or unprovable belief. His was a scientific approach to prayer, which yields direct results, direct experience. To thousands all over the world, he taught that spiritual science — yoga, the science of the soul — the definite methods of inner communion whereby each soul can experience its oneness with the Divine.*

"Be still, and know that I am God." These words from Psalms describe the purpose of yoga. In the inner quietude resulting from deep meditation, each person may find a personal connection with God. Then prayer truly becomes dynamic — an intimate, loving exchange between the soul and its Creator in the sanctuary of silence within.

Paramahansa Yogananda's many books, and his collected talks and essays, contain numerous passages about the way to make prayer effective. In this small volume we have compiled a representative sampling. For those who are just embarking upon an interior life of the Spirit, here is inspiration and definite guidance with which to begin. For those who have already incorporated a program of prayer and meditation into their daily lives, this guide will bring a refocusing and deepening of their relationship with the Divine.

The hallmark of Paramahansa Yogananda's teaching is that God is not remote or unapproachable. Indeed, that Divine One is "the nearest of the near, dearest of the dear, closer than the closest — just

---

* These scientific techniques of meditation taught by Paramahansa Yogananda are available in a home-study series of lessons from Self-Realization Fellowship.

behind our thoughts and feelings, just behind the words with which we pray."

As Paramahansaji shows in the selections in this book, if we devote even a little time each day to prayer and meditation, the Infinite Father–Mother–Friend becomes a living, enlightening Presence in our lives — bringing strength, guidance, renewal, healing.

That is my prayer for you, the reader; and I know it would be Paramahansaji's as well.

Los Angeles
January 1998

Prayer Is a Demand
of the Soul

—◠◡◠—

Enter the quietness of your soul

The temple of God is within your soul. Enter into this quietness and sit there in meditation with the light of intuition burning on the altar. There is no restlessness, no searching or striving there. Come into the silence of solitude....

—⟊—

Enter the innermost sanctuary of the soul. ...Remember and realize the forgotten image of God within you.

—⟊—

Each of us is a child of God. We are born of His spirit, in all its purity and glory and joy. That heritage is unassailable....The Bible says:

"Know ye not that ye are the temple of God, and that the Spirit of God dwelleth in you?" Always remember: your Father loves you unconditionally....

We need not run away to the jungle to seek Him. We can find Him in this jungle of daily life, in the cave of inner silence.

—⁓—

Even if you do no more than pray sincerely to Him, His great joy will eventually come upon you.

—⁓—

True prayer is an expression of the soul, an urge from the soul. It is a hunger for God that arises from within, expressing itself to Him ardently, silently.

—ɯ—

Constantly, inwardly, talk to Him; then He cannot remain away from you.

—ɯ—

The Lord is the Mother of all mothers, the Father of all fathers, the One Friend behind all friends. If you always think of Him as the nearest of the near, you will witness many wonders in your life. "He walks with me and He talks with me and He tells me I am His own."

—ɯ—

WHEN NO HUMAN AID CAN HELP

There are two ways in which our needs can be taken care of. One is the material. For example, when we have ill health we can go to a doctor for medical treatment. But a time comes when no human aid can help. Then we look to the other way, to the Spiritual Power, the Maker of our body, mind, and soul. Material power is limited, and when it fails, we turn to the unlimited Divine Power. Likewise with our financial needs; when we have done our best, and still it is inadequate, we turn to that other Power....

Our endeavor must be not only to acquire financial security and good health, but to seek out the meaning of life. What is it all about? When we are hit with difficulties we react upon our environment first, making whatever material adjustments we believe may help. But when we come to the point of saying, "Everything I have tried so far has failed; what to do next?" we start to think hard about a solution. When we think deeply enough, we find an answer within. This is one form of answered prayer.

—◦◦◦—

When chronic diseases and sufferings are beyond the control of human care; when the power of human methods fails to cure ills, physical or mental, revealing its limitations, then we must ask God to help—He who is unlimited in power.

—◦◦◦—

GOD WILL RESPOND TO YOUR LOVING DEMANDS

God is not a mute unfeeling Being. He is love itself. If you know how to meditate to make contact with Him, He will respond to your loving demands. You do not have to plead; you can demand as His child.

—⚬—

I prefer the word "demand" to "prayer," because the former is devoid of the primitive and medieval conception of a kingly tyrant-God whom we, as beggars, have to supplicate and flatter.

—⚬—

Prayer is a demand of the soul. God did not make us beggars; He created us in His image. The Bible and Hindu scriptures declare it. A beggar who goes to a rich home and asks for alms receives a beggar's share; but the son can have anything he asks from his wealthy father. Therefore we should not behave like beggars. Divine ones such as Christ, Krishna, and Buddha did not lie when they said we are made in the image of God. Yet we see that some people have everything, seemingly born with a silver spoon in their mouth, whereas others seem to attract failure and troubles. Where is the image of God in them? The power of Spirit lies within each one of us; the question is how to develop it.

—m—

Change your status from a beggar to a child of God

The secret of effective prayer is to change your status from beggar to child of God; when you appeal to Him from that consciousness, your prayer will have both power and wisdom.

—◊—

In John 1:12 we find written: "But as many as received Him, to them gave He power to become the sons of God, even to them that believe on His name." The ocean cannot be received in a cup unless the cup is made as large as the ocean. Likewise, the cup of human concentration and human faculties must be enlarged in order to comprehend God. *Receiving* denotes capacity acquired by self-development; it is different from mere belief.

—⚊—

All those who know how to receive Him can realize the divinity sleeping within them by expanding the powers of the mind. Being children of God, we have potential dominion over all things in His universe, even as He has.

—⚊—

IF WE ARE GOD'S CHILDREN, WHY DO WE HAVE SORROW AND SUFFERING?

Why is it that many of our wishes are not fulfilled, and that many of God's children suffer intensely? God, with His divine impartiality, could not make one child better than another. He originally made all souls alike, and in His image. They also received the greatest gifts of God: freedom of the will, and power to reason and to act accordingly.

Somewhere, sometime in the past, [they] have broken the various laws of God, and accordingly have brought about lawful results....

Man has misused this God-given independence and thus has brought upon himself ignorance, physical suffering, premature death, and other ills. He reaps what he sows. The law of cause and effect [karma] applies to all lives.

—⚬—

God, though all-powerful, does not act unlaw-fully or arbitrarily merely because one prays. He has given independence to man, who does with it what he pleases. To forgive human shortcomings so that man can continue his misbehavior without consequences would mean that God contradicts Himself—disregards the law of cause and effect as applied to the law of action—and handles human lives, not according to the laws created by Himself, but according to His whim. Nor can God be moved by flattery or by praise to change the course of His im-mutable laws. Must we then live without the intercession of the grace and mercy of God, and remain helpless victims of human frailties?

Must we then inevitably face the fruits of our actions as if by preordination or so-called fate?

No! The Lord is both law *and* love. The devotee who with pure devotion and faith seeks the unconditional love of God, and who *also* brings his actions into harmony with divine law, will surely receive the purifying, mitigating touch of God.

—◆—

The Divine Power of Its own accord wants to help you; you don't have to coax. But you do have to use your will to demand as His child, and to behave as His child.

—◆—

[Real devotees] know that even if they have not been able to give up bad habits they can bring

God closer and closer by constantly calling upon Him and expecting Him to be present at all times — to take part in their daily lives as well as to respond to them in their moments of prayer. They know that all things are possible to God, and that most understanding lies beyond the intellect. When the devotee insistently demands the assistance and presence of God, lovingly visualizing Him and believing in His omnipresence, then the Lord will reveal Himself in some form. With the dawning of the light of His revelation, the darkness of evil habits will automatically be banished to reveal the untainted soul.

—ᨆ—

DO NOT IDENTIFY YOUR IMMORTALITY WITH HUMAN HABITS

If you have deep devotion for God, you can ask Him anything. Every day I bring new questions to Him, and He answers me. He is never offended by any sincere query we put to Him. Sometimes I even scold Him for starting this creation: "Who is going to suffer the karma for all the evils in this drama? You, the Creator, are free from karma. Why, then, did You subject us to this misery?" I think He feels very sad for us. His desire is to take us back, but He cannot do so without our cooperation and self-effort.

—⁓—

What is done by ourselves can be undone by ourselves.

—⊶⊷—

What are you afraid of? You are an immortal being. You are neither a man nor a woman, as you may think, but a soul, joyous, eternal. Do not identify your immortality with human habits....Even in the midst of exacting trials, say: "My soul is resurrected. My power to overcome is greater than all my trials, because I am a child of God."

—⊶⊷—

Let no one call you a sinner. God made you in His image. To deny that image is the greatest sin against yourself....Darkness may reign in a cave for thousands of years, but bring in the light, and the darkness vanishes as though it had never been. Similarly, no matter what your defects, they are yours no longer when you bring in the light of goodness.

—⁓—

When my trials become very great, I first seek understanding in myself. I don't blame circumstances or try to correct anybody else. I go inside first. I try to clean the citadel of my soul to remove anything that obstructs the soul's all-powerful, all-wise expression. That is the successful way to live.

—⁓—

Wrap yourself in the thought of God. His holy Name is the Power of all powers. Like a shield it deflects all negative vibrations.

—⁓—

Our relationship with God is not a cold impersonal one

Our relationship with God is not a cold impersonal one, like that between employer and employee. We are His children. He *has* to listen to us! There is no way that we can get away from the fact that we are His children. We are not merely creatures created by Him; we are a part of Him. He made us princes, but we have chosen to become slaves. He wants us to become princes once more, to return to our Kingdom. But no one, having renounced his divine heritage, will regain it without effort. We are made in His image, but we have somehow forgotten that truth. We have succumbed to the delusion that we are mortal beings, and we must sunder the veil of that delusion with the dagger of wisdom.

—⟨⟨⟨—

The world's various religions are based more or less on the *beliefs* of man. But the true basis of religion should be a science that all devotees may apply in order to reach our one Father—God. Yoga is that science.

—⟨⟨⟨—

We have come down from God, and we must reascend to Him. We have seemingly become separated from our Father, and we must consciously reunite with Him. Yoga teaches us how to rise above the delusion of separation and realize our oneness with God. The poet Milton wrote of the soul of man and how it might regain paradise. That is the purpose and goal of Yoga—to regain the lost paradise of soul consciousness by which man knows that he is, and ever has been, one with Spirit.

—⁂—

If you live with the Lord, you will be healed of the delusions of life and death, health and sickness. Be in the Lord. Feel His love. Fear nothing. Only in the castle of God can we find protection. There is no safer haven of joy than in His presence. When you are with Him, nothing can touch you.

—⁂—

Remain in the castle of His presence....Carry within you a portable heaven.

—⁂—

THERE IS A RIGHT WAY TO PRAY

In the past you may have been disappointed that your prayers were not answered. But do not lose faith. In order to find out if prayers work or not, you must have in your mind an initial belief in the power of prayer.

Your prayers may have gone unanswered because you chose to be a beggar. Also, you should know what you may legitimately ask of your Heavenly Father. You may pray with all your heart and power to own the earth, but your prayer will not be granted, because all prayers connected with material life are limited; they have to be. God will not break His laws to satisfy whimsical desires. But there is a right way to pray.

—∿—

We must lovingly demand as sons of God and not as beggars. Every begging prayer, no matter how sincere, limits the soul. As sons of God, we must believe that we *have* everything the Father has. This is our birthright. Jesus realized the truth, "I and my Father are one." That is why he had dominion over everything, even as his Father had. Most of us beg and pray without first establishing, in our own minds, our divine birthright; that is why we are limited by the law of beggary. We do not have to beg, but to *reclaim* and *demand* from our Father that which we, through our human imagination, thought to be lost.

It becomes necessary at this stage to destroy the wrong thought of ages — that we are frail human beings.

—⁓—

KNOW YOURSELF AS A SOUL,
A CHILD OF GOD

Through deep meditation you know yourself as a soul, a child of God, made in His image.

—⚹—

You have been in a state of hallucination, thinking you are a helpless mortal....Every day you should sit quietly and affirm, with deep conviction: "No birth, no death, no caste have I; father, mother, have I none. Blessed Spirit, I am He. I am the Infinite Happiness." If you again and again repeat these thoughts, day and night, you will eventually realize what you really are: an immortal soul.

—⚹—

AFFIRM THAT WHICH YOU ARE

Don't behave like a cringing mortal being. You are a child of God!

—⁂—

Affirm that you are a child of God, and dwell on what Jesus said: "I and my Father are one."

—⁂—

Our inner assertion of spiritual identity is sufficient to operate the law for fulfillment of prayers. This law has been utilized by saints of all lands. From the depths of his own experience, Christ was able to give us this glorious assurance:

"If ye have faith, and doubt not...if ye shall say unto this mountain, Be thou removed, and be thou cast into the sea, it shall be done. And all things whatsoever ye shall ask in prayer, believing, ye shall receive."

—◆—

"I believe in God; why doesn't He help me?"

Belief in God and faith in God are different. A belief is valueless if you don't test it and live by it. Belief converted into experience becomes faith. That is why the prophet Malachi told us: "Prove me now herewith, saith the Lord of hosts, if I will not open you the windows of heaven, and pour you out a blessing, that there shall not be room enough to receive it."

—\m/—

Faith, or the intuitive experience of all truth, is present in the soul. It gives birth to human hope and the desire to achieve....Ordinary human beings know practically nothing of this intuitive faith that is latent in the soul, which is the secret wellspring of all our wildest hopes.

—⚬⚬⚬—

Faith means knowledge and conviction that we are made in the image of God. When we are attuned to His consciousness within us, we can create worlds. Remember, in your will lies the almighty power of God. When a host of difficulties comes and you refuse to give up in spite of them; when your mind becomes "set," then you will find God responding to you.

—⚬⚬⚬—

Faith has to be cultivated, or rather uncovered within us. It is there but has to be brought out. If you watch your life you will see the innumerable ways in which God works through it;

your faith will thus be strengthened. Few people look for His hidden hand. Most men consider the course of events as natural and inevitable. They little know what radical changes are possible through prayer!

—⟋⟍—

FAITH BRINGS PROOF OF GOD'S RESPONSE

God does respond when you deeply pray to Him with faith and determination. Sometimes He answers by dropping a thought in the mind of another person who can fulfill your desire or need; that individual then serves as God's instrument to bring about the desired result. You don't realize how wonderfully this great power works. It operates mathematically. There is no "if" about it. And that is what the Bible means by faith: it is *proof* of things unseen.

—⁂—

TRY TO EXPERIENCE YOUR
SPIRITUAL CONVICTIONS

The practice of religion has come to a point where very few try to make their spiritual thoughts a matter of experience....Most persons become self-satisfied about what they have read of Truth, without ever having experienced it.

—⁓—

When you try to experience your spiritual convictions another world begins to open up to you. Don't live in a false sense of security, believing that because you have joined a church you will be saved. You yourself have to make the effort to know God. Your mind may be satisfied that you are very religious, but unless your consciousness is satisfied with direct answers to your prayers, no amount of formal religion can save you. Of what benefit is praying to God if He does not answer? Difficult though it is to obtain His response, it can be done. To assure your ultimate arrival in heaven, you must test the power of your prayers until you have made them effective.

—〰—

TEST THE POWER OF
YOUR PRAYERS

Some persons might protest, saying, "I know my prayers are answered, for I hear God talking to me. I have demonstrated His response to my prayers." The thing is, are you sure that your prayers actually reached God, and that He consciously responded to them? What is the proof? Suppose you have prayed for healing and that you have become well. Do you know whether your cure is due to natural causes, or to medicine, or to your own or another's prayers that brought help from God? Sometimes there is no causal relation between the prayer and the cure. You might have been healed even if you had not prayed. This is the reason why we should find out whether we may scientifically employ the law of cause and effect through prayer. The sages of India found that God responds to law. Those who have experienced this response have said that all people who conform to the law may test and experience it for themselves.

—〰—

If scientists got together and only prayed for inventions, would they get them? No. They have to apply God's laws. So how can a church or temple bring you God just by blind prayer or ceremony?

—〰—

God cannot be "bribed," by gifts or penances or special ceremonies alone, to change His law arbitrarily; nor does He respond to blind prayer or out of partiality. He may be moved only by man's cooperation with the law, and by love: love *is* law. When man has shut the windows of his life indefinitely to God's rays of health, power, and wisdom, it is man who must make the effort to reopen these windows to let in the freely offered, waiting to enter, healing light of the Lord.

—◆—

We must think, meditate, affirm, believe, and realize daily that we are sons of God — and behave accordingly! This realization may take time, but we must begin with the right method, rather than gamble with the unscientific beggary of prayers and consequently be subject to disbelief, doubts, or the jugglery of superstition. It is only when the slumbering ego perceives itself not as a body, but as a free soul or son of God, residing in and working through the body, that it can rightfully and lawfully demand its divine rights.

—◆—

Inner Concentration:
Prelude to True Prayer

REMEMBER THE
INDWELLING LORD

Develop the consciousness that God is with you.

—⁓—

The Lord seems distant only because your attention is directed outward to His creation and not inward to Him. Whenever your mind wanders in the maze of myriad worldly thoughts, patiently lead it back to remembrance of the indwelling Lord. In time you will find Him ever with you — a God who talks with you in your own language, a God whose face peeps at you from every flower and shrub and blade of grass. Then you shall say: "I am free! I am clothed in the gossamer of Spirit; I fly from earth to heaven on wings of light." And what joy will consume your being!

—〜—

Divine Spirit, bless us that within our hearts we speak only of Thee evermore. No matter what we say with our tongues, our hearts will ever be repeating Thy name.

—〜—

Once when I was meditating I heard His voice, whispering: "Thou dost say I am away, but thou didst not come in. That is why thou dost say I am away. I am always in. Come in and thou wilt see Me. I am always here, ready to greet thee."

—〜—

"When thou prayest, enter into thy closet"

The Sanskrit word for faith is wonderfully expressive. It is *visvas*. The common literal rendering, "to breathe easy; have trust; be free from fear," does not convey the full meaning. Sanskrit *svas* refers to the motions of breath, implying thereby life and feeling. *Vi* conveys the meaning of "opposite; without." That is, he whose breath, life, and feeling are calm, he can have faith born of intuition; it cannot be possessed by persons who are emotionally restless. The cultivation of intuitive calmness requires unfoldment of the inner life. When developed sufficiently, intuition brings immediate comprehension of truth. You can have this marvelous realization. Meditation is the way.

Meditate with patience and persistence. In the gathering calmness, you will enter the realm of soul intuition. Throughout the ages, those beings who attained enlightenment were those who had recourse to this inner world of God-communion. Jesus said: "When thou prayest, enter into thy closet, and when thou hast shut thy door, pray to thy Father which is in secret; and thy Father which seeth in secret shall reward thee openly." Go within the Self, closing the door of the senses and their involvement with the restless world, and God will reveal to you all His wonders.

—⚬⚬⚬—

How did the saints first find God?

How did seekers first find Him? As the beginning step, they closed their eyes to shut out immediate contact with the world and matter, so they could concentrate more fully on discovering the Intelligence behind it. They reasoned that they could not behold God's presence in nature through the ordinary perceptions of the five senses. So they began to try to feel Him within themselves by deeper and deeper concentration. They eventually discovered how to shut off all five senses, thus temporarily doing away entirely with the consciousness of matter. The inner world of the Spirit began to open up. To those great ones of ancient India who undeviatingly persisted in these inner investigations, God finally revealed Himself.

Thus the saints gradually began to convert their conceptions of God into perceptions of Him. That is what you must do also, if you would know Him.

—⚮—

IN YOUR SILENCE GOD'S
SILENCE CEASES

Sensations pouring in through the sensory nerves keep the mind filled with myriad noisy thoughts, so that the whole attention is toward the senses. But God's voice is silence. Only when thoughts cease can one hear the voice of God communicating through the silence of intuition. That is God's means of expression. In your silence God's silence ceases. He speaks to you through your intuition. For the devotee whose consciousness is inwardly united with God, an audible response from Him is unnecessary—intuitive thoughts and true visions constitute God's voice. These are not the result of the stimuli of the senses, but the combination of the devotee's silence and God's voice of silence.

God has been with us all the time, talking to us; but His voice of silence has been drowned by the noisiness of our thoughts: "Thou didst love me always, but I heard Thee not." He has always been near; it is we who have been wandering away from His consciousness.

In spite of our indifference and pursuit of sense pleasures, still God is loving us, and always will. To know this, we must withdraw our thoughts from sensations and be silent within. Silencing the thoughts means tuning them in to God. That is when true prayer begins.

—⚬—

Don't think of anything but the Spirit when you are praying

When we pray we should try our utmost to concentrate our whole attention on God, instead of saying "God, God, God" and letting our minds dwell on something else. An aunt of mine had the habit of saying her prayers on beads. She could almost always be seen busily fingering her beads. But she approached me one day and confessed that although she had been doing this for forty years, God had never answered her prayers. No wonder! Her "prayers" were hardly more than a nervous physical habit. Don't think of anything but the Spirit when you are praying.

Blind repetition of demands or affirmations, without concomitant devotion or spontaneous love, makes one merely a "praying Victrola," which does not know what its prayer means. Grinding out prayers vocally and mechanically, while inwardly thinking of something else, does not bring response from God. A blind repetition, taking the name of God in vain, is fruitless. Repeating a demand or prayer over and over again, mentally or orally, and with deepening attention and devotion, spiritualizes the prayer, and changes conscious, believing repetition into superconscious experience.

—ᴍ—

WHICH PRAYER WILL MOST QUICKLY DRAW THE DIVINE BELOVED?

Give God the gems of prayer lying deep in the mine of your own heart.

—⟋⟍—

One should not rely on a book on love when he meets his beloved, but should use the spontaneous language of his heart. If one uses another's language of love in demands addressed to God, he must make the words his own, by thoroughly understanding and dwelling upon their meaning, and applying to them the utmost concentration and love; even as it is not amiss when a lover addresses his beloved in the language of a great poet, and enlivens those words with his own love and feeling.

—⟋⟍—

Love God with all your heart...

The highest commandments given to man are to love God with all your heart, and with all your soul, and with all your mind, and with all your strength; and secondly, to love your neighbor as yourself. If you follow these, everything will come in its own way, and in the right way. It is not enough just to be a strict moralist — stones and goats do not break moral laws; still, they do not know God. But when you love God deeply enough, even if you are the greatest of sinners, you will be transformed and redeemed. The great saint Mirabai said, "To find the Divine One, the only indispensable is love." That truth touched me deeply.

All the prophets observe these two foremost commandments. Loving God with all your heart means to love Him with the love that you feel for the person who is dearest to you — with the love of the mother or father for the child, or the lover for the beloved. Give that kind of unconditional love to God. Loving God with all your soul means you can truly love Him when through deep meditation you know yourself as a soul, a child of God, made in His image. Loving God with all your mind means that when you are praying, your whole attention is on Him, not distracted by restless thoughts. In meditation, think only of God; don't let the mind wander to everything else but God. That is why yoga is important; it enables you to concentrate. When by yoga you withdraw the restless life force from the sense nerves and become interiorized in the thought of God, then you are loving Him with all of your strength — the whole of your being is concentrated in Him.

What if one doesn't feel love for God?

Sitting in the silence trying to feel devotion may often get you nowhere. That is why I teach scientific techniques of meditation. Practice them and you will be able to disconnect the mind from sensory distractions and from the otherwise ceaseless flow of thoughts. By Kriya Yoga* one's consciousness functions on a higher plane; devotion to the Infinite Spirit then arises spontaneously in man's heart.

—⚶—

* This advanced spiritual science of interiorized God-communion, which originated millenniums ago in India, is taught by Paramahansa Yogananda in the *Self-Realization Fellowship Lessons.* (Publisher's Note)

WHERE MOTION CEASES, THERE BEGINS THE PERCEPTION OF GOD

Learn to be still in body and mind, for where motion ceases, there begins the perception of God.

—⁂—

Your trouble in meditation is that you don't persevere long enough to get results. That is why you never know the power of a focused mind. If you let muddy water stand still for a long time, the mud will settle at the bottom and the water will become clear. In meditation, when the mud of your restless thoughts begins to settle, the power of God begins to reflect in the clear waters of your consciousness.

—⁂—

The moon's reflection cannot be seen clearly in ruffled water, but when the water's surface is calm a perfect reflection of the moon appears. So with the mind: when it is calm you see clearly reflected the moonèd face of the soul. As souls we are reflections of God. When by meditation techniques we withdraw restless thoughts from the lake of the mind, we behold our soul, a perfect reflection of Spirit, and realize that the soul and God are One.

—⚍—

KNOW THE SCIENCE OF BROADCASTING YOUR PRAYERS AND RECEIVING GOD'S ANSWERS

As a broken microphone cannot broadcast a message, so a restless mind cannot transmit prayers to God.

———

By skillful use of the techniques of meditation, repair your mental microphone. When you feel calm, your mental microphone is in working order; this is the time to broadcast your first and foremost loving demand: "Father, make me realize again that Thou and I are One." Aloud, then in a whisper, and finally just mentally affirm, "Father, Thou and I are one."

———

Do not give up after one or two tries if God doesn't seem to respond. You cannot get an answer merely by calling someone through a microphone and then running away. So don't stop after one or two mental broadcasts; with conscious effort and zeal, go on talking mentally to God, with ever-increasing longing in your heart.

—⁂—

Pray intelligently, with a bursting soul—not loudly, but mentally—without displaying to anyone what is happening within. Pray with the utmost devotion, knowing God is listening to every word flowing from your heart.

—⁂—

If after repeated attempts you still do not see God or hear His knock at the gate of your heart, do not be discouraged. For a long time you have been running away from Him, hiding in the marshes of the senses. The noises of your own rowdy passions, and of the flight of your heavy footsteps in the world of matter, have made you unable to hear His call within. Stop. Be calm. Pray steadfastly, and out of the silence will loom the Divine Presence.

—◊—

When you feel a bursting thrill of joy expanding in your heart and your whole body, and it continues to increase even after meditation, you have received the one sure proof that God has answered through the devotion-tuned radio of your heart. The heart, which is the center of feeling, and the mind, which is the center of reason, must be one-pointedly concentrated in order for your mind-radio message to reach God, and for you to receive His answer.

The longer and deeper you meditate and pray to Him, the more deeply you will feel and be conscious of the expanding joy in your heart. Then you will know without doubt that there is a God and that He is ever-existing, ever-conscious, omnipresent, ever-new Joy. That is the time to ask Him: "Father, now, today, all days, all tomorrows, every instant, in sleep, in wakefulness, in life, in death, in this world and in the beyond, remain Thou with me as the consciously responding Joy of my heart."

After praying, ask if you wish for healing of the body, for prosperity, or whatever other temporal aid your discriminative wisdom indicates is needed.

—ɯ—

III

Know What to Pray For

WHAT IS THE BEST PRAYER?

Say to the Lord: "Please tell me Thy will." Don't say: "I want this and I want that," but have faith that He knows what you need. You will see that you get much better things when He chooses for you.

—⁓—

Determine honestly whether or not your prayer is legitimate. Do not ask God for things that are quite impossible in the natural order of life. Ask only for true necessities. And know the difference between "necessary necessities" and "unnecessary necessities."...Cut out desires for needless possessions. Concentrate only on your real needs. Your greatest necessity is God. He will give you not only your "necessary necessities," but your "unnecessary necessities" as well. He will satisfy your every desire when you are one with Him. Your wildest dreams will come true.

—∿—

The things you need in life are those that will help to fulfill your dominant purpose. Things you may *want* but not *need* may lead you aside from that purpose. It is only by making everything serve your main objective that success is attained. Consider whether fulfillment of the goal you have chosen will constitute success. What *is* success? If you possess health and wealth, but have trouble with everybody (including yourself), yours is not a successful life. Existence becomes futile if you cannot find happiness. When wealth is lost, you have lost a little; when health is lost, you have lost something of more consequence; but when peace of mind is lost, you have lost the highest treasure.

—ᴟ—

THE MORE YOU CONCENTRATE ON EXTERNALS, THE LESS HAPPY YOU WILL BE

The mule that carries a bag of gold on its back doesn't know the value of that load. Likewise, man is so absorbed in toting the burden of life, hoping for some happiness at the end of the trail, that he does not realize he carries within him the supreme and everlasting bliss of the soul. Because he looks for happiness in "things," he doesn't know he already possesses a wealth of happiness within himself.

GOD IS NOT SOMETHING YOU HAVE TO EARN

After a while creature comforts become burdens, pleasures no longer, because you find it is hard work to take care of them. Thus you "pay" for everything you get except divine blessedness. For that you have only to sit still and ask your Heavenly Father. If I thought I had to earn God I wouldn't try; as a son I have a right to know Him. If you ask your right from the Father, He will give it to you. To those devotees who urge, He comes. That is what He wants.

—m—

"Sustain me according to Thy will"

It is not wrong to tell the Lord that we want something. But it shows greater faith if we simply say: "Heavenly Father, I know that Thou dost anticipate my every need. Sustain me according to Thy will." If a man is eager to own a car, for instance, and prays for it with sufficient intensity, he will receive it. But possession of a car may not be the best thing for him. Sometimes the Lord denies our little prayers because He intends to bestow on us a better gift. Trust more in God. Believe that He who created you will maintain you.

It is a fact that sometimes your most fervent prayers and desires are your greatest enemies. Talk sincerely and justly with God, and let Him decide what is right for you. If you are receptive, He will lead you, He will work with you. Even if you make mistakes, don't be afraid. Have faith. Know that God is with you. Be guided in everything by that Power. It is unfailing.

—〜—

Pray to God for guidance

The time to pray to God for guidance is after you have meditated and felt that inner peace and joy; that is when you have made the divine contact. If you think you have a need, you can then place it before God and ask whether it is a legitimate prayer. If you feel inwardly that your need is just, then pray: "Lord, You know that this is my need. I will reason, I will be creative, I will do whatever is necessary. All I ask of You is that You guide my will and creative abilities to the right things that I should do."

SEEK HIS GUIDANCE WITHIN

Go to God; pray and cry to Him until He shows the workings of His laws to you and guides you. Remember, greater than a million reasonings of the mind is to sit and meditate upon God until you feel calmness within. Then say to the Lord, "I can't solve my problem alone, even if I thought a zillion different thoughts; but I can solve it by placing it in Your hands, asking first for Your guidance, and then following through by thinking out the various angles for a possible solution." God does help those who help themselves. When your mind is calm and filled with faith after praying to God in meditation, you are able to see various an-swers to your problems; and because your mind is calm, you are capable of picking out the best solution. Follow that solution, and you will meet with success. This is applying the science of religion in your daily life.

—⁓—

"Seek ye first the kingdom of God and all these things shall be added unto you"

Most people reason that if they first acquire prosperity and material security, they can then think of God. But such procrastination only carries one in a circle of unending dissatisfaction. God must be found first. He is the greatest need in your life, for He is the Source of lasting happiness and security. If just once the consciousness of His presence comes to you, then you will know what true happiness is. If just once you have this actual contact with God, you will realize that when you have Him, the universe is at your feet. God is your provider; He must be with you always.

If you think of God in deepest meditation, if you love Him with all your heart, and feel completely at peace in His presence, without wishing for anything else, the divine magnetism of God will attract unto you everything you ever dreamed about, and much more. In every department of my life I have demonstrated this truth: If you love God for His own Self, not because of what He can give you; and if you are completely attracted by His divine magnetism, that power from Him goes out of your own heart and mind, and by your slightest little wish, you will attract unto yourself the fulfillment of that desire. If you have unconditional love for God, He drops thoughts in others' brains, and they become instruments to fulfill even your unspoken desires.

—◠◠◠—

Every prayer that you utter represents a desire. But when you find God, all desires vanish, and there is no need for prayer. I don't pray. That may seem a strange thing to say, but when the Object of your prayer is with you all the time, you no longer have need to pray. In fulfillment of the wish or prayer for Him lies joy eternal.

—⦿—

I tell you truthfully that all my questions have been answered, not through man but through God. He *is*. He *is*. It is His spirit that talks to you through me. It is His love that I speak of. Thrill after thrill! Like gentle zephyrs His love comes over the soul. Day and night, week after week, year after year, it goes on increasing — you don't know where the end is. And that is what you are seeking, every one of you. You

Have a Clear
Concept of God

—ɯ—

When the right method is applied, it scientifically bears results

To know exactly how and when to pray, according to the nature of our needs, is what brings the desired results. When the right method is applied, it sets in motion the proper laws of God; the operation of these laws scientifically bears results.

—m—

First you must have a right concept of God — a definite idea through which you can form a relationship with Him — and then you must meditate and pray until that mental conception becomes changed into actual perception.

WHAT IS GOD?

God is Eternal Bliss. His being is love, wisdom, and joy. He is both impersonal and personal, and manifests Himself in whatever way
He pleases. He appears before His saints in the
form each of them holds dear: a Christian sees
Christ, a Hindu beholds Krishna or the Divine
Mother, and so on. Devotees whose worship
takes an impersonal turn become conscious of
the Lord as an infinite Light or as the wondrous
sound of *Aum,* the primal Word, the Holy
Ghost. The highest experience man can have is
to feel that Bliss in which every other aspect of
Divinity — love, wisdom, immortality — is fully
contained. But how can I convey to you in
words the nature of God? He is ineffable, in-
describable. Only in deep meditation shall you
know His unique essence.

—⧗—

Many people don't like to think of the Lord ⸙
personal; they feel that an anthropomorphic
conception is limiting. They consider Him to be
Impersonal Spirit, All-Power, the Intelligent
Force that is responsible for the universe.

But if our Creator is impersonal, how is it
that He has created human beings? We are
personal; we have individuality. We think, feel,
will; and God has given us not only the power
to appreciate the thoughts and feelings of others
but to respond to them. The Lord is surely not
devoid of the spirit of reciprocity that animates
His own creatures. When we permit it, our
Heavenly Father can and will establish a personal relationship with each one of us.

—⧗—

You can see Him from tonight if you make up your mind

During every little period of leisure, plunge your mind into the infinite thought of Him. Talk to Him intimately; He is the nearest of the near, the dearest of the dear. Love Him as a miser loves money, as an ardent man loves his sweetheart, as a drowning person loves breath. When you yearn for God with intensity, He will come to you.

—〜—

Last summer I stopped at a monastery, where I met one of the priests. He was a wonderful soul. I asked him how long he had been on the spiritual path as a monk. "About twenty-five years," he replied.

Then I asked: "Do you see Christ?"

"I don't deserve it," he answered. "Maybe after death he will visit me."

"No," I assured him, "you can see him from tonight if you make up your mind." Tears were in his eyes, and he remained silent.

You must pray intensely. If you sit night after night practicing meditation and crying to God, the darkness will be burned up, and you will see the Light behind this physical light, the Life behind all life, the Father behind all fathers, the Mother behind all mothers, the Friend behind all friends, the Element behind all elements, the Power behind all powers.

—⁓—

Pray With Dynamic
Will Power

—m—

RIGHT PRAYER INCLUDES
WILL POWER

Lazy people think that just by virtue of prayer God will listen to them and fulfill their desires. But it is necessary to exercise will power, to strive to tune it with the divine will. When your will revolves continually around one definite purpose, it becomes dynamic will. This is the quality of will power possessed by Jesus and by all other great sons of God.

—⁓—

Many people say we should not exercise our will to change conditions, lest we interfere with God's plan. But why would God give us will if we are not to use it? I once met a fanatical man who said he did not believe in using will power because it developed the ego. "You are using a lot of will now to resist me!" I replied. "You are using it to talk, and you are obliged to use your will to stand, or walk, or eat, or go to the movies, or even to go to sleep. You will everything you do. Without will power you would be a mechanical man." Nonuse of the will is not what Jesus meant when he said: "Not as I will, but as Thou wilt." He was demonstrating that man must learn to bend his will, which is governed by desires, to the will of God. Therefore right prayer, when it is persistent, is will.

—✺—

CONTINUAL MENTAL WHISPERS DEVELOP DYNAMIC POWER TO ACCOMPLISH YOUR WILL

When you want to see a special show, or to buy a dress or a car you have admired, is it not true that no matter what else you may be doing your mind is continually thinking how you can get those things? Until you fulfill your strong desires, your mind will not rest; it ceaselessly works toward fulfilling those desires....

Mental whispers develop dynamic power to reshape matter into what you want. You do not realize how great is the power of the mind. When your mind and will are attuned to the Divine Will you do not have to move a finger in order to create changes on earth. The divine law will work for you. All the salient accomplishments of my life have been achieved through that power of mind in tune with the will of God. When that divine dynamo is on, whatever I am wishing has to come to pass.

—⚬—

Keep applying will and positive affirmation until you make thought work for you. Thought is the matrix of all creation; thought created everything. If you hold on to that truth with indomitable will, you can materialize any thought. There is nothing that can gainsay it. It was by that kind of powerful thought that Christ rebuilt his crucified body; and it is what he referred to when he said, "Therefore I say unto you, What things soever ye desire, when ye pray, believe that ye receive them, and ye shall have them."

—⚬—

In the seclusion of concentrated thought lies hidden the factory of all accomplishment. Remember that. In this factory continuously weave your will pattern for attaining success over opposing difficulties. Exercise your will continuously. During the day and at night you have many opportunities to work in this factory, if you do not waste your time. At night I withdraw from the world's demands and am by myself, an absolute stranger to the world; it is a blank. Alone with my will power, I turn my thoughts in the desired direction until I have determined in my mind exactly what I wish to do and how to do it. Then I harness my will to the right activities and it creates success. In this way I have effectively used my will power many times.

—⁓—

WHEN THE "CAN'T" DISAPPEARS FROM YOUR MIND, DIVINE POWER COMES

You must believe in the possibility of what you are praying for. If you want a home, and the mind says, "You simpleton, you can't afford a house," you must make your will stronger. When the "can't" disappears from your mind, divine power comes. A home will not be dropped down to you from heaven; you have to pour forth will power continuously through constructive actions. When you persist, refusing to accept failure, the object of will must materialize. When you continuously work that will through your thoughts and activities, what you are wishing for has to come about. Even though there is nothing in the world to conform to your wish, when your will persists, the desired result will somehow manifest. In that kind of will lies God's answer; because will comes from God, and continuous will is divine will. A weak will is a mortal will. As soon as trials and failure cut it off, it loses its connection with the dynamo of the Infinite. But behind human will is the divine will that can never fail. Even death has no power to deter divine will. The Lord will definitely answer that prayer behind which the will force is continuous.

—◊—

"IF YE SHALL SAY UNTO THIS MOUNTAIN, BE THOU REMOVED..."

When you make up your mind to do good things, you will accomplish them if you use dynamic will power to follow through. No matter what the circumstances are, if you go on trying, God will create the means by which your will shall find its proper reward. This is the truth Jesus referred to when he said: "If ye have faith, and doubt not...if ye shall say unto this mountain, Be thou removed, and be thou cast into the sea, it shall be done."

—※—

Study the lives of the saints. That which is easy to do is not the way of the Lord. That which is difficult to do is His way! Saint Francis had more troubles than you could imagine, but he didn't give up. One by one, by the power of mind, he overcame those obstacles and became one with the Master of the Universe. Why shouldn't you have that kind of determination?

—⚊—

How can we develop will?

Every day undertake something that is difficult for you, and try to do it. Though you fail five times, keep on, and as soon as you have succeeded in that direction, apply your concentrated will on something else. You will thus be able to accomplish increasingly greater things. Will is the instrument of the image of God within you. In will lies His limitless power, the power that controls all the forces of nature. As you are made in His image, that power is yours to bring about whatever you desire: You can create prosperity; you can change hatred into love. Pray until body and mind are completely subjugated; then you will receive God's response.

—✺—

MEAN BUSINESS WITH GOD

Most people are merely wishing when they express desire for healing and the belief that God can heal them. In reality, they pray with disbelief in their hearts or with a sense of futility, thinking God will not heed their prayers; or they pray and do not wait to find out if their prayers have reached God.

—⁂—

Talking to Him a little while and then forgetting will never bring His response. God is "hard to get" because not everyone "means business" with Him. The technique of prayer is usually ineffectual because most prayers are not deep or devotional enough.

CRY UNTIL THE DIVINE MOTHER COMES

Prayer in which your very soul is burning with desire for God is the only effectual prayer. You have prayed like that at some time, no doubt; perhaps when you wanted something very badly, or urgently needed money—then you burned up the ether with your desire. That is how you must feel for God.

—◈—

When you know a thing is right, why shouldn't you go after it? Why shouldn't you cry for the Lord until the skies are shaken with your prayers?...Remember, it is the naughty baby who gets the mother's attention. The easily pacified infant is soon satisfied with toys. But the naughty baby wants the mother only, and goes on crying until she comes.

Do you want toys or God?

—w—

BOTH!
God First!

GIVE THE DIVINE MOTHER A CALL
FROM YOUR SOUL

"Give my Mother a soul call; She can't remain hidden anymore." Close your eyes, think of God, and give the Divine Mother a call from your soul. This you can do any time, anywhere. No matter what else you may be doing, you can mentally converse with God: "My Lord, I am looking for You. I don't want anything but You alone. I long to be with You always. You made me in Your image; and my home is with You. You have no right to keep me away from You. Maybe I have done wrong, tempted by delusions of Your cosmic play; but because You are my Mother, my Father, my Friend, I know You will forgive me and take me back. I want to go Home. I want to come to Thee."

—⟋⟍—

Every night when you sit to meditate, pray to
God unceasingly. Tear the silence with your
longing. Cry to God as you would cry to your
mother or to your father: "Where are You?
You made me; You gave me intelligence to seek
You. You are in the flowers, in the moon, and
in the stars; must You remain hidden? Come to
me. You must! You must!" With all the concentration of your mind, with all the love of
your heart, tear at the veils of silence again and
again. As constant churning brings hidden but-
ter out of milk, churn the ether with the ladle of
your devotion and it shall produce God.

—⟋⟍—

ASK WITH ALL YOUR HEART, AGAIN AND AGAIN

Do not rest until He answers. Ask with all your heart, again and again: "Reveal Thyself! Reveal Thyself! The stars may be shattered, the earth may be dissolved, yet my soul shall cry unto Thee, 'Reveal Thyself!'" The inertia of His silence will be broken by the steady, persistent hammering of your prayers. At last, like the invisible earthquake, He will suddenly make Himself manifest. The walls of silence holding back the reservoir of your consciousness will tremble and crumble, and you will feel that you are flowing like a river into the Mighty Ocean, and you will say to Him: "I am now one with Thee; whatever Thou hast, the same have I."

VI

Reclaim Your Inner Sanctuary

—◊◊◊—

In the quietness
of the soul

When God does not respond to your prayers, it is because you are not in earnest. If you offer Him dry imitation prayers, you cannot expect to claim the Heavenly Father's attention. The only way to reach God through prayer is by persistence, regularity, and depth of earnestness. Cleanse your mind of all negation, such as fear, worry, anger; then fill it with thoughts of love, service, and joyous expectation. In the sanctum of your heart there must be enshrined one power, one joy, one peace — God.

—⁂—

God in His infinite mercy gives to us His joy, His inspiration, true life, true wisdom, true happiness, and true understanding through all the various experiences of our lives. But the glory of God is revealed only in the quietness of the soul....

The more you concentrate on the outside, the less you will know of the inner glory of the everlasting joy of Spirit. The more you concentrate within, the less you will have of difficulties without.

—⁕—

Just one thought may redeem you. You don't realize how effectively your thoughts work in the ether. I realize my true nature.

—⁕—

Every thought we think sets up a particular subtle vibration....When you mentally utter the word God, and keep on repeating that thought within, it sets up a vibration that invokes the presence of God.

—⚏—

Saturate everything with the thought of God. Realize that all that exists is centered in God.

—⚏—

He cannot be bribed at any time, yet it is easy to move Him with sincerity, persistency, concentration, devotion, determination, and faith.

—⚏—

Remove from your mind all doubt that God will answer

You must remove from your mind all doubt that God will answer. Most people don't get any response because of their disbelief. If you are absolutely determined that you are going to attain something, nothing can stop you. It is when you give up that you write the verdict against yourself. The man of success doesn't know the word "impossible."

PRAY WITH PATIENCE AND FAITH

Suppose you have a mortgage on your home and you cannot meet it. Or there is a certain job you want. In the silence that comes after meditating deeply, concentrate with unswerving will on the thought of your need. <u>Do not keep looking for the result.</u> If you sow a seed in the ground and then take it out every once in a while to see if it is growing, it will never sprout. Similarly, if every time you pray you look for a sign that the Lord is granting your wish, nothing will happen. Never try to test God. Just go on praying unceasingly. Your duty is to bring your need to God's attention, and to do your part in helping God to bring that desire to fruition. For example, in chronic diseases, do your best to help promote healing, but know in your mind that ultimately God alone can help.

Take that thought with you into meditation every night, and with all your determination pray; suddenly one day you will find the disease gone.

—⁊⁊⁊—

After sowing the demand-seed in the soil of faith, do not dig it up now and then in order to examine it, or it will never germinate to fulfillment. Sow your demand-seed in faith, and water it by repeated daily practices in demanding rightly. Never be discouraged if results are not forthcoming immediately. Stand firm in your demands, and you will regain your lost divine heritage; and then, and then only, will the Great Satisfaction visit your heart. Demand until you establish your divine rights. Demand unceasingly that which belongs to you, and you will receive it.

—⚏—

Even true devotees think sometimes that God
does not answer their prayers. He does answer
silently, through His laws; but until He is absolutely sure of the devotee He will not answer
openly, He will not talk to the devotee. The
Lord of Universes is so humble that He does
not speak, lest in so doing He influence the
devotee's use of free will to choose or reject
Him. Once you know Him, there is no doubt
that you will love Him. Who could resist the
Irresistible? But you have to prove your unconditional love for God in order to know Him.
You have to have faith. You have to *know* that
even as you pray He is listening to you. Then
He will make Himself known to you.

—⚏—

IN THE CAVE OF INNER SILENCE, YOU SHALL FIND THE WELLSPRING OF WISDOM

He who is mentally undefeated is the one who finds God within the temple of his heart. No matter what your obstacles, this you can do: In the secret sanctuary of your heart you can seek God; and you can love Him with all your heart. Whenever there is a little time between duties, retire to the cave of silence within. You won't find silence amidst crowds. Seek time to be alone; and in the cave of inner silence, you shall find the wellspring of wisdom.

—⁓—

FIND SANCTUARY IN THE INNER TEMPLE OF SILENCE

———

Be silent and calm every night for at least half an hour, preferably much longer, before you retire, and again in the morning before starting the day's activity. This will produce an un-daunted, unbreakable inner habit of happiness that will make you able to meet all the trying situations of the everyday battle of life. With that unchangeable happiness within, go about seeking to fulfill the demands of your daily needs.

—⟊—

Wherever your mind is, that is where you will spend your time.

—⟊—

When tigers of worries, sickness, and death are chasing you, your only sanctuary is the inner temple of silence. The spiritually deep man lives day and night in a calm interior silence into which neither menacing worries nor even the crash of colliding worlds can intrude....

What joy awaits discovery in the silence behind the portals of your mind, no human tongue can tell. But you must convince yourself; you must meditate and create that environment. Those who deeply meditate feel a wonderful inner quiet. This stillness within should be maintained even when in the company of other people. What you learn in meditation, practice in activity and conversation; let no one dislodge you from that calm state. Hold on to your peace....In your inner temple of silence receive God with your awakened intuition.

God is in the heart and soul of every being. And when you open within yourself the secret temple in your heart, then with the all-knowing intuition of the soul you shall read the book of life. Then, and only then, will you contact the living God. And you will feel Him as the very essence of your being. Without this feeling in your heart, there will be no answer to your prayers. You may attract what your positive actions and good karma permit you to have; but to receive conscious response from God, you must first attain divine attunement with Him.

—⁓—

IMMERSE YOURSELF IN THE PEACE OF GOD

Mentally call to God with all the fervor and sincerity of your hearts. Consciously invoke Him in the temple of silence; and in deeper meditation, find Him in the temple of ecstasy and bliss. Chant with the consciousness that God is here. Through your thoughts and feelings, send Him your love with all your heart, mind, soul, and strength. Through the intuition of your soul feel the manifestation of God bursting through the clouds of your restlessness as great peace and joy. Peace and joy are the voices of God that have long slumbered beneath your ignorance, ignored and forgotten in the din of human passions.

The kingdom of God is just behind the darkness of closed eyes, and the first gate that opens to it is your peace. Exhale and relax, and feel this peace spread everywhere, within and without. Immerse yourself in that peace.

Inhale deeply. Exhale. Now forget your breath. Repeat after me:

"Father, hushed are the sounds of the world and the heavens. I am in the temple of quietness. Thine eternal kingdom of peace is spread tier upon tier before my gaze. May this infinite kingdom, long hidden behind the darkness, remain manifest within me. Peace fills my body; peace fills my heart and dwells within my love; peace within, without, everywhere. God is peace. I am His child. I am peace. God and I are one."

—⚊⚊—

In God is your real home

When we are in tune with God, we will hear His voice: "I have loved thee through the ages; I love thee now; and I shall love thee until thou comest Home. Whether thou knowest it or not, I shall always love thee."

He speaks to us in silence, telling us to come Home.

———〰———

You can't fail to reach God ultimately. It is foolish to ask, "Will I be able to get into the kingdom of heaven?" There is no other place you can stay, for that is your real home. You don't have to earn it. You are already God's child, made in His image. You have only to tear away the mask of the human being and realize your divine birthright.

In the temple of silence He will give you the gift of Himself

You are all gods, if you only knew it. Behind the wave of your consciousness is the sea of God's presence. You must look within. Don't concentrate on the little wave of the body with its weaknesses; look beneath. Close your eyes and you see the vast omnipresence before you, everywhere you look. You are in the center of that sphere, and as you lift your consciousness from the body and its experiences, you will find that sphere filled with the great joy and bliss that lights the stars and gives power to the winds and storms. God is the source of all our joys and of all the manifestations in nature....

Awaken yourself from the gloom of igno-rance. You have closed your eyes in the sleep of delusion. Awake! Open your eyes and you shall behold the glory of God — the vast vista of God's light spreading over all things. I am telling you to be divine realists, and you will find the answer to all questions in God....

You must claim your divine birthright. Your constant prayer, your boundless determination, your unceasing desire for God, will make Him break His tremendous vow of silence, and He will answer you. Above all, in the temple of silence He will give you the gift of Himself.

—◊◊◊—

THE PRAYER THAT SHOULD BE FIRST IN EVERY HEART

God is real, and He can be found in this life.

In men's hearts there are many prayers — for money, fame, health — prayers for all manner of things. But the prayer that should be first in every heart is the prayer for God's presence. Silently and surely, as you walk on the path of life, you must come to the realization that God is the only object, the only goal that will satisfy you; for in God lies the answer to every desire of the heart....

Your soul is a divine temple of God. The darkness of mortal ignorance and limitations must be driven out of that temple. It is wonderful to be in the consciousness of the soul — fortified, strong!

Be afraid of nothing. Hating none, giving love to all, feeling the love of God, seeing His presence in everyone, and having but one desire — for His constant presence in the temple of your consciousness — that is the way to live in this world.

—⚏—

ABOUT THE AUTHOR

PARAMAHANSA YOGANANDA (1893–1952) is widely regarded as one of the preeminent spiritual figures of our time. Born in northern India, he came to the United States in 1920, where for more than thirty years he taught India's ancient science of meditation and the art of balanced spiritual living. Through his acclaimed life story, *Autobiography of a Yogi,* and his numerous other books, Paramahansa Yogananda has introduced millions of readers to the perennial wisdom of the East. Under the guidance of one of his closest disciples, Sri Mrinalini Mata, his spiritual and humanitarian work is carried on by Self-Realization Fellowship, the international society he founded in 1920 to disseminate his teachings worldwide.